RENOIR

RENOIR

A RETROSPECTIVE

Edited by Nicholas Wadley

BEAUX
ARTS
EDITIONS

ISBN 0-88363-962-9

This book was designed and produced by
JOHN CALMANN AND KING LTD, LONDON

Designer Robert Updegraff
Typeset by Composing Operations Ltd, England
Printed in China

The excerpts in this book are reproduced by kind permission of the copyright owners, as follows:

Jean Renoir, *Renoir, My Father* (translated by Randolph and Dorothy Weaver) © 1962 by Jean Renoir. Reprinted by permission of A.D. Peters & Co Ltd. and Little, Brown and Company.

Renoir: An Intimate Record, by Ambroise Vollard, translated by Harold L. Van Doren and Rudolph T. Weaver. © 1925 and renewed 1953 by Alfred A. Knopf Inc. Reprinted by permission of the publisher.

Paul Valéry, *The Collected Works*, edited by Jackson Mathews, Vol. 12: *Degas, Manet, Morisot*, translated by David Paul, Bollingen Series 45. © 1960 Princeton University Press. Excerpts reprinted with permission of Princeton University Press and Routledge, Kegan Paul, London.

John Rewald, *Studies in Impressionism.* Reproduced by permission of Thames & Hudson Ltd, London.

A. Tabarant, *Pissarro.* Reproduced by permission of The Bodley Head, London.

Jacques-Emile Blanche, *La Pêche aux Souvenirs*, © Flammarion, Paris, 1949.

Gerd Muehsam, *French Painters & Paintings from the Fourteenth Century to Post-Impressionism: A Library of Art Criticism*, © The Frederick Ungar Publishing Company.

Camille Pissarro, *Letters to his son, Lucien*, edited by John Rewald with the assistance of Lucien Pissarro. Translated by Lionel Abel. Copyright © 1943 by Pantheon Books Incorporated. Reprinted by permission of the publisher.

Teodor de Wyzewa, *Peintres de jadis et d'aujourd'hui.* © Librairie Perrin, Paris.

Maurice Denis, *Theories, 1890-1910.* © Editions Lanore, H. Laurens L.T.

Octave Mirbeau, *Renoir*, © Bernheim Jeune, Editor, 1913.

Gustave Geffroy, *La Vie Artistique*, E. Dentu, Paris, 1894. © Editions Fayard, Paris.

Julie Manet, *Journal (1893-1899).* © Klincksieck, Paris, 1979.

Léonce Bénédite, *Madame Charpentier and her Children* from The Burlington Magazine, Vol. XII, December, 1907.

Walter Pach, *Queer Thing, Painting.* © Harper & Row, New York, 1938. Reprinted by permission of the publisher.

Cassatt & her Circle, Selected Letters, edited by Nancy M. Mathews. Courtesy of Abbeville Press, New York.

Matisse: His Art and His Public by Alfred H. Barr, Jr. English translation copyright © 1951, The Museum of Modern Art, New York. All rights reserved. Reprinted by permission.

Françoise Gilot and Carleton Lake, *Life with Picasso.* © McGraw-Hill, New York and Thomas Nelson & Sons, London. Reprinted by permission.

Clive Bell, *Since Cézanne*, © the author's estate and Chatto & Windus: The Hogarth Press Ltd

Extract from Maurice Denis, *Du symbolisme au classicisme. Théories*, © Hermann, Paris, 1964.

André Lhote, 'Renoir et l'Impressionisme' (1920), in *Parlons Peinture*, Paris 1936. © Editions Denoël, Paris.

Extract reprinted by permission of Faber and Faber Ltd from *The Life and Opinions of Walter Richard Sickert* edited by Robert Emmons.

Clive Bell, *Landmarks in Nineteenth Century Painting*, © the author's estate and Chatto & Windus: The Hogarth Press Ltd

Charles Fogdal, *Essais critiques sur l'Art Moderne*, Librairie Stock, Paris 1927. © Editions Stock.

Christian Zervos, *Le retour au sujet est-il probable?* © Editions "Cahiers d'Art", 1931.

Extract reprinted by permission of Faber and Faber Ltd from *The Meaning of Art* by Herbert Read.

P. Heron, *The Changing Forms of Art.* Reproduced by permission of Routledge, Kegan Paul, London.

Art and Culture: Critical Essays by Clement Greenberg. Copyright © 1961 by Clement Greenberg. Reprinted by permission of Beacon Press, Boston and Thames and Hudson Ltd, London.

Keith Vaughan, catalogue for retrospective exhibition. Permission Whitechapel Art Gallery.

Kenneth Clark, *The Nude: A Study in Ideal Form.* No. 2 in the A.W. Mellon Lectures in the Fine Arts, Bollingen Series XXXV. © 1956, 1984 renewed by the Trustees of the National Gallery of Art. Excerpts reprinted with permission of Princeton University Press and John Murray Ltd, London.

John Berger, *Permanent Red.* Reprinted by permission of the author and Methuen Ltd, London.

Philip James, *Henry Moore on Sculpture.* Copyright © 1966, 1971, by Philip James and Henry Moore. Reprinted by permission of Viking Penguin, New York and Macdonald, London.

Kenneth Clark, *Civilisation.* Reprinted by permission of John Murray Ltd, London, and Harper & Row, New York.

Joel Isaacson, *The Crisis of Impressionism 1878-1882*. Reprinted by permission of the University of Michigan Museum of Art.

Old Mistresses: Women, Art and Ideology by Roszika Parker and Griselda Pollock. Copyright © 1981, Roszika Parker and Griselda Pollock. Reprinted by Pantheon Books, a division of Random House Incorporated.

Tamar Garb, 'Renoir and the natural woman', The Oxford Art Journal, Volume 8, 1985. Reprinted by permission of Oxford University Press.

Professor Lawrence Gowing, *Renoir*, ACGB catalogue, 1985. Extract reprinted by permission of Professor Gowing and the Arts Council.

Fred Orton, 'Reactions to Renoir keep changing', The Oxford Art Journal, Volume 8, 1985. Reprinted by permission of Oxford University Press.

Excerpts transcribed from 'Renoir, What is Painting for, anyway?' Reproduced by permission of the British Broadcasting Corporation, Howard Hodgkin, Bridget Riley and David Sylvester.

Full information for each excerpt is given in the Bibliographical Index, pp.10-11.

Jacket: Detail of *Dance at Bougival*, 1883. Museum of Fine Arts, Boston (Picture Fund). See colorplate 84

CONTENTS

Bibliographical Index

Full details of each source book are listed at the first reference, and in an abbreviated form of author and date thereafter. Where a later edition has been used, the original date of publication is given first in parentheses. Translations are by Paula Clifford, Judith Landry or Nicholas Wadley unless otherwise indicated.

References in the margin notes on the texts to "Daulte" followed by a number are to Françoise Daulte, *Auguste Renoir, Catalogue raisonné, I, Figures 1860–1890*, Durand-Ruel, Lausanne 1971.

p. 49 Georges Rivière, *Renoir et ses Amis*, Floury, Paris, 1921, pp. 3–6.

p. 51 Théodore Duret, *Manet and the Impressionists*, Grant Richards, London, 1910, pp. 159–60.

p. 51 Jean Renoir, *Renoir, My Father*, (1958), Collins, London, 1962, pp. 57–67.

p. 55 Ambroise Vollard, *Renoir, An Intimate Record*, Knopf, New York, 1925, pp. 24–29.

p. 57 Albert André, *Renoir*, (1919). Crés, Paris, 1928, pp. 54–55.

p. 57 Vollard 1925, pp. 30–31.

p. 59 Lionello Venturi, *Les Archives de l'Impressionisme*, Durand-Ruel, Paris, New York, 1939. I, p. 30.

p. 59 *Cahiers d'Aujourd'hui*, Paris, No. 2, January 1921.

p. 60 Venturi 1939, II, p. 276.

p. 60 *L'Opinion Nationale*, Paris, June 20, 1868.

p. 60 *La Presse*, Paris, June 23 1868.

p. 61 Venturi 1939, II, pp. 281–82.

p. 61 Trans. Paul Valéry, *Degas, Manet, Morisot*, Routledge & Kegan Paul, London, 1960, pp. 129–33.

p. 63 Venturi 1939, II, p. 283.

p. 64 Rivière 1921, pp. 14–20.

p. 74 Rewald, *Studies in Impressionism*, Thames & Hudson, London, 1985, pp. 9–25.

p. 75 Rivière 1921, pp. 61, 68–71.

p. 77 Venturi 1939, II, pp. 288 ff.

p. 78 Trans. Charles S. Moffett et al., *The New Painting, Impressionism 1874–1886*, Fine Arts Museums of San Francisco, 1986, p. 141.

p. 80 Vollard 1925, pp. 62–63.

p. 80 Ambroise Vollard, *Recollections of a Picture Dealer*, Constable, London, 1936, p. 169.

p. 80 Rivière 1921, pp. 121–26.

p. 84 Venturi 1939, II, pp. 286–87.

p. 84 Trans. John Rewald, *History of Impressionism*, (1946), Museum of Modern Art, New York, 1973, pp. 368–70.

p. 85 Trans. Charles S. Moffett et al., 1986, pp. 184–85.

p. 86 Rivière 1921, pp. 65–68.

p. 88 Rivière 1921, pp. 77–78.

p. 105 Rivière 1921, pp. 89–91.

p. 106 Venturi 1939, II, pp. 308 ff. Trans. B.E. White (ed.), *Impressionism in Perspective*, Prentice Hall, New Jersey, 1978, pp. 8–9 and Judith Landry.

p. 108 *Chronique des Arts et de la Curiosité*, Paris. April 14 1877.

p. 108 Venturi 1939, II, p. 322.

p. 109 Venturi 1939, II, pp. 291–92.

p. 110 Trans. Charles S. Moffett et al., 1986, pp. 234–36.

p. 112 Venturi 1939, II, pp. 336 ff.

p. 114 Rivière 1921, pp. 167–76.

p. 118 A. Tabarant, *Pissarro*, John Lane & Bodley Head, London 1925, pp. 39–40.

p. 119 Philippe Burty, *La République Française*, Paris, May 27 1879.

p. 119 Castagnary, *Le Siècle*, Paris, June 1879.

p. 120 J.K. Huysmans, *L'Art Moderne*, Charpentier, Paris, 1883, pp. 58–59.

p. 120 Reprinted in Théodore Duret, *Histoire des Peintres Impressionistes*, Floury, Paris 1922, pp. 27–28.

p. 129 Venturi 1939, II, pp. 334–38.

p. 132 *L'Impressionnisme*, Galerie Braun, Paris, p. 11.

p. 132 Renoir 1962, pp. 187–90.

p. 136 Paul Gachet, *Deux Amis des Impressionistes*, Musées Nationaux, Paris, 1956, pp. 166–67.

p. 136 Venturi 1939, II, p. 277.

p. 137 Renoir 1962, pp. 128–29.

p. 137 Jacques-Emile Blanche, *La Pêche aux Souvenirs*, Flammarion, Paris, 1949: pp. 443–45.

p. 138 M. Florisoone, "Renoir et la famille Charpentier: lettres inédites", *L'Amour de l'Art 19*, Paris, 1938, p. 36.

p. 139 Venturi 1939, I, pp. 116–17.

p. 140 M. Schneider, "Renoir: lettres sur l'Italie", *L'âge d'or – etudes I*, 1945, p. 97 ff.

p. 141 M. Drucker, *Renoir*, Tisné, Paris, (1944) 1945, pp. 103–4.

p. 143 Venturi 1939, I, pp. 115–22.

p. 156 Rewald 1973, pp. 469–70.

p. 156 J.K. Huysmans, 1883, pp. 256–66.

p. 157 Trans. Charles S. Moffett et al. 1986, pp. 411–17.

p. 158 Venturi 1939, I, pp. 64–65.

p. 159 Venturi 1939, I, pp. 125–26.

p. 159 Venturi 1939, I, pp. 126–27; 267–68.

p. 160 Rivière 1921, pp. 197–201.

p. 163 Vollard 1925, pp. 118–23.

p. 164 Venturi 1939, I, pp. 127–29. Trans. from L. Nochlin (ed.), *Impressionism and Post-Impressionism 1874–1904* . . . New Jersey, 1966, pp. 45–47.

p. 165 *La France*, Paris, December 8 1884.

p. 165 Renoir 1962, p. 224.

p. 166 Trans. Gerd Muehsam (ed.), *French Painters and Paintings from the Fourteenth Century to Post-Impressionism: A Library of Art Criticism*, Frederick Ungar Pub., N.Y. 1970, pp. 511–12.

p. 167 Venturi 1939, I, pp. 131–32.

p. 167 D. Rouart (ed.), *The Correspondence of Berthe Morisot*, Lund Humphries, London, 1957. p. 130.

p. 168 Camille Pissarro, *Letters to his son Lucien*, Kegan Paul, Trench, Trubner, London, 1943, pp. 107–8, 120.

p. 168 Vincent Van Gogh: *The Complete Letters*, Thames & Hudson, London, 1958, Vol II, pp. 556–59, 566–67.

p. 169 François Daulte, *Renoir I*, Durand-Ruel, Lausanne 1977, p. 53.

p. 170 D. Rouart (ed.), 1957, pp. 144–45.

p. 179 Rivière 1921, pp. 202–3.

p. 180 Gustave Geffroy, *Claude Monet, sa Vie, son Oeuvre*, (1924), Macula, Paris, 1980, pp. 261–62.

p. 181 Téodor de Wyzewa, *Peintres de jadis et d'Aujour-d'hui*, Perrin, Paris, 1903, pp. 371–76.

p. 183 Arsène Alexandre, "Renoir", Durand-Ruel, Paris, May–June, 1892.

p. 183 Maurice Denis, *Théories*, Rouart & Watelin, Paris, 1920, p. 19.

p. 184 Octave Mirbeau, *Renoir*, Bernheim-Jeune, Paris, 1913, p. 10.

p. 184 D. Rouart (ed.), 1957, p. 172.

p. 185 Renoir 1962, pp. 279–80.

p. 186 Renoir 1962, pp. 236–38.

p. 187 Gustave Geffroy, *La Vie Artistique*, 3rd series, E. Dentu, Paris, 1894, pp. 111–26.

p. 192 Renoir 1962, pp. 255–57.

p. 193 Renoir 1962, pp. 268–70.

p. 209 Julie Manet, *Journal (1893–1899)*, Klincksieck Paris, 1979.

p. 212 Manet 1979.

p. 213 Jeanne Baudot, *Renoir*, Editions Littéraires, Paris, 1949, pp. 11–30.

p. 215 Thadée Natanson, *Peints à leur Tour*, Albin Michel, Paris, 1948, pp. 28–32.

p. 216 Baudot 1949, pp. 40–43.

p. 217 Renoir 1962, pp. 301–12.

p. 219 Baudot 1949, pp. 49–50.

p. 220 Venturi 1939, I, pp. 169–96.

p. 222 Wyzewa 1903, pp. 376–87.

p. 234 E.L. Duval, *Téodor de Wyzewa, Critic Without a Country*, Librairie Droz, Geneva, 1961, pp. 139–40.

p. 234 Venturi 1939, I, p. 182.

p. 235 Trans. White (ed.), 1978, pp. 21–24.

p. 237 *The Burlington Magazine*, vol XII, December 1907, pp. 130–35.

p. 241 Renoir 1962, pp. 388–90.

p. 243 Walter Pach, *Queer Thing, Painting*, New York, 1938, pp. 104–6.

p. 246 Venturi 1939, I p. 107.

p. 247 J. Meier-Graefe, "Auguste Renoir", Floury, Paris, 1912.

p. 257 Mirbeau 1913, n.p.

p. 258 N.M. Mathews (ed.), *Cassatt and her Circle, Selected Letters*, N.Y. 1984, pp. 308, 313, 315.

p. 259 Vollard 1925, pp. 148–52.

p. 260 Alfred Barr, *Matisse, his Art and his Public*, Museum of Modern Art, New York, 1951, p. 196.

p. 261 Françoise Gilot/Carleton Lake, *Life with Picasso*, Penguin, London, p. 260.

p. 262 Albert André (1919) 1928.

p. 276 Baudot 1949, pp. 96–99.

p. 278 Clive Bell, *Since Cézanne*, Chatto & Windus, London, 1922, pp. 66–73.

p. 280 Roger Fry, *Vision and Design*, (1920), Pelican, London, 1961, pp. 209–13.

p. 282 Maurice Denis, *Théories du Symbolisme au Classicisme*, Hermann, Paris, 1964, p. 124 ff.

p. 284 André Lhote, *Parlons Peinture*, Denoël A. Steele, Paris, 1936, pp. 164–70.

p. 288 Trans. Gerd Muehsam (ed.), 1970, pp. 514–15.

p. 288 Geffroy (1924) 1980, pp. 279–82.

p. 301 W.R. Sickert, *The Life and Opinions of W.R.S.*, Faber, London, 1941.

p. 301 Clive Bell, *Landmarks in Nineteenth Century Painting*, Chatto & Windus, London 1927, pp. 174–82.

p. 311 *Cahiers d'Art, 3*, Paris, 1931, pp. 117–26.

p. 313 Herbert Read, *The Meaning of Art*, Faber, London, 1931, pp. 127–29.

p. 314 Robert Rey, *La Renaissance du Sentiment Classique*, Les Beaux Arts, Paris, 1931.

p. 339 Albert C. Barnes & Violette de Mazia, *The Art of Renoir*, Barnes Foundation, Merion, Pa., 1935, pp. 39–40.

p. 340 John Rewald, *Renoir Drawings*, (1946), Thomas Yoseloff, New York, 1958, pp. 8–13.

p. 341 P. Heron, *The Changing Forms of Art*, Routledge & Kegan Paul, London, 1955, pp. 121–22.

p. 342 Clement Greenberg, *Art and Culture*, Beacon Press, Boston, 1950, pp. 46–49.

p. 344 *Keith Vaughan, Retrospective Exhibition*, catalogue, Whitechapel Art Gallery, London, March–April 1962, p. 30.

p. 345 Kenneth Clark, *The Nude*, (1956), Penguin, London, 1960, pp. 154–61.

p. 348 Renoir 1962.

p. 358 John Berger, *Permanent Red*, Methuen, London, 1960, pp. 199–200.

p. 359 Philip James (ed.), *Henry Moore on Sculpture*, Viking Press, New York, 1966, pp. 195–97.

p. 360 Kenneth Clark, *Civilisation*, John Murray/ B.B.C., London, 1969, pp. 342–43.

p. 360 *The Crisis of Impressionism 1878–1882*, catalogue, University of Michigan Museum of Art, 1979–80, pp. 32–39.

p. 371 Rozsika Parker and Griselda Pollock, *Old Mistresses; Women, Art and Ideology*, Routledge & Kegan Paul, London, 1981, pp. 121–23.

p. 372 *The Oxford Art Journal*, Oxford, Vol. 8, No. 2, 1985, pp. 4–14.

p. 373 *Renoir*, catalogue, Arts Council of Great Britain, Hayward Gallery, London, 1985, pp. 30–33.

p. 375 *The Oxford Art Journal*, Oxford, Vol. 8, No. 2, 1985, pp. 28–33.

p. 377 B.B.C. Television, London, 1985.

ACKNOWLEDGEMENTS

I am very grateful to those friends and colleagues who have given me suggestions and advice in compiling the texts: to Martha Kapos, Jasia Reichardt, Stefan Themerson, David Thompson, Gerard Wilson, Christopher Yetton and particularly to Steven Bury, senior librarian at Chelsea School of Art, London, for his unfailing and freely-given help; to Paula Clifford and, especially, Judith Landry for all their work on the translations, as well as to Barbara Wright, Blanche Bronstein and Anita Seal for their guidance; finally, to Elisabeth Ingles, Susan Dixon, Annabel Hood and Robert Updegraff for their editorial, research and design skills in putting the book together with me.

As far as the sources are concerned, I and the publishers are grateful to all those publishers and authors who have given permission for their texts and translations to be reprinted here and to all those museums and private collectors who have allowed works to be reproduced. I am particularly indebted to the research in two recent publications: Barbara E. White's *Renoir, his Life, Art and Letters* (Abrams, New York, 1984 and Flammarion, Paris, 1985) and *Renoir*, the exhibition catalog by John House and his colleagues (Arts Council of Great Britain, 1985). Like all writers on Impressionist painting, I also owe an important debt to John Rewald for his founding work on the subject.

NICHOLAS WADLEY

PUBLISHER'S NOTE
Inconsistencies of spelling, punctuation and style occur in some excerpts because we have reproduced the originals exactly. Where translations have been made specially for this book, normal American spelling and punctuation have been used.

CHRONOLOGY

1841

FEBRUARY 25. Renoir is born at Limoges, the sixth of seven children of Léonard and Marguerite (née Merlet) Renoir (respectively tailor and dressmaker). He is baptized Pierre-Auguste the same day.

1844–54

His family moves to Paris, Renoir is educated at a Catholic school, sings in the choir of St. Eustache. He receives voice training from the young Gounod, is introduced to opera and, for a while, professional training as a singer is considered.

1854–59

Is apprenticed for four years to a porcelain painter and subsequently works as a jobbing decorator for a manufacturer of blinds, as a painter of fans and as a mural-painter of café-bars.

Takes drawing lessons from the sculptor Callouette at a school of drawing and decorative arts.

1860–64

Is registered to copy paintings in the Louvre and prints in the Bibliothèque Impériale.

1861: fellow student there from 1862 of Monet, Sisley, Bazille. Draws from the antique, master prints, paintings and the model. His examination record is mostly undistinguished, his best being fifth (out of 27) in a perspective examination; 10th (out of 106) and 20th (out of 80) in drawing examinations.

Visits the Louvre with Fantin-Latour.

Meets Pissarro and Cézanne at this time and – during summer painting trips to Fontainebleau – Diaz, Courbet, Corot, Daubigny. Is befriended by the painter Jules Le Coeur.

Sends two paintings to the Salon: *A Nymph with a Faun* is rejected in 1863, *La Esmeralda* is accepted in 1864. (Both were subsequently destroyed.)

1865

SPRING. His parents move to the suburbs (Ville d'Avray).

He stays frequently with Sisley in Paris and with Jules Le Coeur in Marlotte, where he meets Lise Tréhot, subsequently his mistress and model.

Shows a portrait of Sisley's father and *Summer Evening* at the Salon.

1866

Stays frequently with Sisley and the Le Coeur family.

JANUARY. Exhibits three paintings in Pau.

SPRING. Submits two paintings to the Salon: *Landscape with Two Figures* is rejected (despite interventions by Corot and Daubigny); a sketch made at Marlotte is accepted, but withdrawn.

JULY. Shares a studio with Bazille (until 1870), joined there briefly by Monet.

1867

SPRING. *Diana* is rejected at the Salon. Signs an (unsuccessful) petition calling for a Salon for the rejected works.

JULY–AUGUST. Spends summer in Chantilly.

1868

JANUARY. With Bazille, moves to a studio near the Café Guerbois, meeting place of Manet and his circle, which they frequent; also meets Degas, Duret, Zola, Burty, Silvestre, etc.

MARCH? Commissioned, via Charles Le Coeur (architect, brother of Jules), to decorate the Paris house of Prince Bibesco (decoration destroyed 1911).

SPRING. *Lise* is accepted at the Salon and well reviewed.

SUMMER. Stays at Ville d'Avray.

1869

SPRING. *Summer* is accepted at the Salon.

JULY–SEPTEMBER. Works with Monet at Bougival during the summer; they paint *La Grenouillère* together.

AUTUMN. Shows two paintings at Galerie Carpentier, Paris.

1870

SPRING. *Bather* and *Woman of Algiers* are accepted at the Salon.

OCTOBER. Is drafted into the cavalry following the outbreak of the Franco-Prussian war; posted to Tarbes, Libourne (where he falls ill) and then to Bordeaux.

NOVEMBER 28. Bazille is killed in action.

1871

SPRING. By April has returned to Paris. During Commune spends time between Paris and Louveciennes, his parents' home.

AUGUST. Stays in Marlotte with Jules Le Coeur.

AUTUMN. Rents a studio and apartment in Rue Notre-Dame-des-Champs, Paris; renews contact with Monet.

1872

MARCH. Is introduced by Monet to Durand-Ruel, who purchases a flower still life and *Pont des Arts*, exhibited later in the year in London.

SPRING. *Parisian Women Dressed as Algériennes* is rejected at the Salon. Signs a petition to the Fine Arts Minister requesting a *Salon des Refusés*.

APRIL. His model Lise marries.

SUMMER. Works with Monet at Argenteuil; they visit Caillebotte.

1873

SPRING. *Ride in the Bois de Boulogne* and a portrait are shown in a *Salon des Refusés*.

MARCH? Through Degas meets Théodore Duret, who purchases *Summer* and *Lise*.

SUMMER. Stays with Monet in Argenteuil.

AUTUMN. Moves apartment to Rue Saint-Georges, where his circle includes Georges Rivière.

1874

APRIL–MAY. Exhibits six paintings in the first show of the *Société anonyme coopérative des artistes peintres, sculpteurs, graveurs, etc* (the first "Impressionist" Exhibition), Boulevard des Capucines, Paris, including *La Loge* and *Parisienne*.

JUNE. Durand-Ruel shows two Renoir paintings in London. His friendship with the Le Coeur family is broken off.

JULY. Stays with the Monet family in Argenteuil, as does Manet.

1875

MARCH. Sells 20 paintings for modest prices at an auction of Impressionist paintings, Hôtel Drouot, Paris. Meets the collector Victor Choquet and the publisher Georges Charpentier. Makes new contacts with critics, writers and patrons through the salons of Mme Charpentier.

DECEMBER 22. Death of Renoir's father at Louveciennes.

Bazille, *The Studio of Bazille, Rue de la Condamine.*
1870. Musée d'Orsay, Paris.

SPRING. Probably is rejected at the Salon.
Is commissioned to copy Delacroix's *Jewish Wedding in Morocco.*

1876
FEBRUARY. Shows two paintings, Société des Amis des Arts, Pau.

APRIL. Shows 15 paintings in the second Impressionist exhibition, Rue le Peletier, Paris, including *Study (Nude in Sunlight)*, a painting of his model Margot.

SUMMER. Working on paintings of Montmartre.

SEPTEMBER. Stays with Alphonse Daudet at Champrosay.
Commissions from the Charpentier family, including a mural.

1877
APRIL. Shows 21 paintings in the third Impressionist exhibition, Rue le Peletier, Paris.

Is instrumental in the founding of the journal *L'Impressioniste,* to which he contributes two articles on the decorative arts.

MAY. Sells 16 works in an auction at the Hôtel Drouot, Paris.

OCTOBER. Meets Gambetta; requests curatorship of a provincial museum.

Friendship with the pastry cook Eugène Murer; attends the Wednesday dinners at his restaurant in the late 1870s.

1878
MAY. *The Cup of Chocolate* is accepted at the Salon.

MAY–JUNE. His illustrations are published in Duret's *Les Peintres Impressionistes* and Zola's *L'Assommoir.*

JUNE. Three Renoir paintings are sold for only 157 francs at the auction of Hoschedé's collection, Hôtel Drouot, Paris.

1879
FEBRUARY. Margot (Alma-Henriette Leboeuf), his model (and maybe mistress) since 1875, dies of smallpox.

APRIL. Does not contribute to the fourth Impressionist exhibition.

MAY–JUNE. *Portrait of Madame Charpentier and her Children, Portrait of Jeanne Samary* and two pastel portraits accepted at the Salon. The Charpentier portrait is well hung and well reviewed in the press.

JUNE–JULY. Paintings and/or pastels and then drawings shown in two exhibitions at the gallery of Georges Charpentier's newly founded journal *La Vie Moderne,* in which Edmond Renoir writes a supportive article.